A BURDEN
AND AN
ACHE

But as he descended the hill, a sadness came upon him, and he thought in his heart:

How shall I go in peace and without sorrow? Nay, not without a wound in the spirit shall I leave this city.

Long were the days of pain I have spent within its walls, and long were the nights of aloneness; and who can depart from his pain and his aloneness without regret?

Too many fragments of the spirit have I scattered in these streets, and too many are the children of my longing that walk naked among these hills, and I cannot withdraw from them without a burden and an ache.

—Kahlil Gibran, THE PROPHET

A BURDEN AND AN ACHE

Clarence McConkey

ABINGDON PRESS

Nashville • New York

A BURDEN AND AN ACHE

Copyright © 1970 by Abingdon Press

ISBN 0-687-04322-0

Library of Congress Catalog Card Number: 72-109681

SET UP, PRINTED, AND BOUND BY THE
PARTHENON PRESS, AT NASHVILLE,
TENNESSEE, UNITED STATES OF AMERICA

For my wife
And my mother
Gentle women in the Faith

CONTENTS

INTRODUCTION

It would be understandable if the reader of this book assumed from the title, or from the opening quotation from Kahlil Gibran, that I think of myself as some kind of special urban missionary or authority on the things of the Inner City. I think of myself in no such way. There are authorities in the Inner City, but I am not among them. The real authorities of the Inner City, the specialists, the technicians, the strategists, are those who have lived in the Inner City from birth. Those for whom I have a burden and an ache are not objects of missionary concern, although they, like all of us, are objects of Christian loving. Since those reflected in the title of this book are suburbanites as well as Inner City residents, small-town citizens as well as urban dwellers, my feelings are more of appreciation and love than they are of missionary concern.

My missionary concern would be ill-advised even if it were a fact, for the Inner City is quite self-reliant in so many important ways. There is a courageous spirit in my part of the city. It is both daring and creative. It is a spirit born of hope and faith—not of despair, as some observers of the Inner City claim. The winds of the spirit blowing through the Inner City are more imaginative and hopeful and uplifting than one can imagine. This spirit is a child of circumstance, but it is nevertheless genuine. It is sometimes brawling, often destructive, frequently cruel. It does not always have

9

direction. But in the Inner City children learn the values of survival, and young people learn what they must do and what they must be, and parents learn what defenses they must construct if they are to make a go of it with their family.

This is the spirit of the Inner City of which I write. It is the spirit of a beautiful people, just now coming to greatness. This is why I cannot withdraw from the Inner City, for to withdraw from it would be to withdraw from those who have loved me, who have taught me, and who support me even now. It is why there is, for all men and women of this city, for children and young people, a burden and an ache. It is a burden of life as it has been. It is an ache of things about to be born.

The Inner City is so many things, it is thought of in so many ways, it is the object of so many efforts and programs, that I think it defies all analysis and all efforts directed toward it. The Inner City is so real, so vital and alive, that I doubt anyone can describe it adequately. I can describe it only as it seems to me.

Of all the insights I have gained in this ministry, that insight which reveals the Inner City to be "protection" stands out most in my mind. It is protection against the hostility and aggression of the rest of the city. The Inner City may have congestion, poor housing, inferior schools, deteriorating streets, insufficient fire and police protection, and inadequate services, but for those who live there it is protection, a place of refuge, a haven of safety. The people of the Inner City know the indifference of politicians in City Hall, the hostility which greets them in Police Court or in Domestic Relations Court, the lack of basic civility in stores, the avarice which shows so clearly at the Loan Company, in automobile showrooms and real estate offices, the deep-seated antagonism of a great many churches. These Inner City people know quite well what they are thought of and so they draw together, a drawing in of life, a search for protection and safety and reassurance.

There is a restlessness about this, however, which we must never misunderstand. There is a pushing out as well as a drawing in, and the spreading of the Inner City in every metropolitan area today is witness to this fact. This pushing out is not an attempt to "take over" something, but rather an attempt to relate to, to communicate with, to be a part of, the rest of the city. Those who push out of the Inner City do so with very little hostility. They are quite ready to change, to adjust, to try to upgrade themselves if they have reason to feel that such giving up and adjusting and trying results in acceptance and respect.

The Inner City is not always black, neither exclusively nor predominantly in a great many cases. Indeed, the central quality of Inner City life is its colorlessness. That is not to say that color is not present in the Inner City, for just the reverse is true. No one sees so much color as in this part of the city. Color abounds here; it enriches and deepens, and not infrequently purifies. Black, white, brown, red, yellow, bronze, and gold all light up the rainbow of the human family in the Inner City. The colorlessness of which I speak has to do with the absence

11

of concern about such color. The intermingling of races, ethnic groups, and cultural stocks here creates a partially colorless society, and while this does not mean that one noses his racial identity in any sense, it does mean that one's racial identity is not an occasion for paranoia.

Thrift was not born in the Inner City but it certainly flourishes there. Among many of these persons thrift means deciding between new shoes at the store or used shoes at Goodwill. It is cold water versus hot water for a bath. It is walking to work or taking a bus. Thrift is swimming for the children at thirty-five cents, or going for a free walk in the park. It is wool versus wash-and-wear. It is preventive dental care against dentures. It is ADC and illicit intercourse with one's own husband, or husband and hungry children. It is sometimes little versus nothing.

Each Sunday morning I preside over an experience of worship into which I enter as worshiper as well as clergyman. It is a high moment in my life to be privileged to offer the call to worship, "The Lord be with you," and to gather back the response, "And with thy spirit." It is in these experiences of proclamation and renewal of the Word that I am constantly reminded of the fundamental nature of my ministry. People often ask me what there is in this ministry that makes me stay here with the risk and the uncertainty. I rather think that question is asked of any person in experimental ministries. I answer that I am not quite sure why I stay in the Inner City. It is certainly true that I am not irreplaceable. Perhaps there is something of the martyr in me. Perhaps, in some hidden way, this life meets a need I have. I do not really know. I tell myself that I am here because I am called here by God. I hope I am not mistaken in this. I do stay in this ministry because I have the hope that someday I will be adequate for it. I stay because I like the people here and because they put up with me even though I fumble and make enormous mistakes.

I give the only kind of ministry I know how to give. That ministry is concern for the people with whom I work and a commitment to tell them as much about Jesus as I know how. It is a ministry which comes from love for persons and the church. Here in the Inner City I see the church at work in so many marvelous ways. For example, each weekday evening in churches and private homes children come to be tutored. Tutoring was born in this city in the Ames Avenue United Church brought into being by a devoted and talented lay couple. This tutoring program for children from the Inner City has been staffed by Catholic students, attended by black children, funded by United Methodists, and directed by a Jewish college student from the University of Pennsylvania. These children from the neighborhood fill the church, sit on the chancel steps, overflow into adjacent homes, lounge on sidewalks and stairways, on the fire escape landing and street curbs.

In one night's labor, the church more than justifies its existence in the Inner City, and provides me with reason enough to continue in this ministry. It is true that I do not always know where to begin or where to stop. The list of needs and possibilities are so great that I do not always know where to draw the line in investing resources. I only know that we are just now beginning a significant ministry in the Inner City.

So I am glad to be here, and I look forward to that time when all those who are a part of this book, and their progeny, will live in dignity and fulfillment. Then the burden and the ache will be gone, and I will live quite contentedly with my memories, and some scars, but with joy and gratitude for such a ministry.

Although the Inner City is not exclusively black, I am sometimes surprised at myself for spending so much time trying to overcome racial prejudice. Negroes certainly do not need me to defend them. They can defend themselves quite well, if indeed they need to be defended at all. And there is no white person in this society who can describe what it is like to be a Negro. You must be black to know what it is like being black. It is blasphemous and a mistake for any white to describe how it feels to be black. Yet I cannot remain silent when Negroes are set upon, ridiculed, robbed, insulted and maligned. Such silence is not within me.

Sometimes whites say to me, "Are the things we hear about Negroes really true? Are they really like that?" I can only reply, "What is it you believe about them." They tell me then the familiar story of Negroes. They are stupid, dull, and lazy. They are dirty and diseased. The men all want to marry white girls. They all want the jobs now held by whites. They let their property run down. They are immoral. They carry knives and razors. They are violent, brawling, and dangerous. This is what

14

some of my white contemporaries believe. When I reply or react, I answer that yes, there are some Negroes like that. There are Negroes who are dirty, lazy, immoral, violent, and dangerous. My friends are right about that.

But these white friends are wrong when they substitute "The Negro" for "Negroes." Whatever characteristic is to be found in blacks is to be found in equal proportion in whites, Orientals, Indians, and all others. The Inner City is cosmopolitan and its members share a great many things. And whatever may be said about blacks must also be said about whites and other ethnic groups. It is this accusation which opens up the enormous gulf between the Inner City and the rest of Metropolis. No one knows how much of the labor and effort of human rights today is directly aimed at bridging the widening gap between the Inner City and the rest of urban life.

Not so long ago I took my family to one of the great seasonal music programs presented by one of the churches of this city. This church, once located in the very heart of the downtown business district, has now relocated to the wide expanse of the western part of the city. The building is an adornment of architecture. Expensive, tasteful, aesthetic, and utilitarian, the building in itself is more than enough to attract the inquiring Christian. It has magnificent choirs, a highly paid staff, property worth millions. Its great spire dominates the skyline and points the worshiper skyward.

My family and I are seated in a high-vaulted nave surrounded by organ, cushioned pews, draperies, and chancel furniture provided by Christians who felt certain their gifts were to the glory of God. At least the brass plates beneath each window would so testify. We sit enchanted while the assembly of musicians renders a monumental classic of sacred music. The voices are powerful and soaring. Somehow, listening to this music, caught up in the swell of a great master, we are taken away from the things of the earth to a world far more celestial. It is a cleansing time, a renewing time, a necessary time, for the seeker after spiritual things.

Then, just as it seems that we are ready to be permanently fixed in the starry heavens of pure delight, an earth voice intrudes to ask for an offering. He explains that, after all, the great metal lighting towers which stand on either side of the chancel were rented for the occasion. In addition to that, some special equipment had to be purchased, a new microphone installed that would do justice to the voice-to-sound chamber relationship, and that the music alone is a major factor. All in all he estimates that the cost of this production, and those are his exact words, will come to something like $1,000, and would everyone be so kind as to help meet those expenses?

Halted between earth and sky I realize that my trip beyond the earth has just been aborted. And I think of the $1,000. One of the churches in my parish has bare light bulbs hanging from the ceiling. The furniture of the Sunday school is old and broken and often repaired. That church spends what little it has for others. I think of the $1,000. I think of all those children who come to the church night after night to be tutored and who sit on sidewalks and on fire escape landings and street curbs because the church building is too small. I think of Rick in his ministry to the young people of our community. Rick is a young Air Force sergeant who drives twenty miles from his base, day after day, to be a part of this work. He gives his time, wears out his car, and dedicates himself completely in his ministry to these young people. I remember all those who come to me for help and are turned away because I do not have money for them. For $1,000 we could buy audio-visual equipment for the tutoring program, repair the sidewalks, buy an old bus, get a better typewriter. For $1,000 we could provide a great many things that so many people need for so many reasons.

My family and I leave the church and drive back to the Inner City. We have been helped by the music we have heard and by the inner contemplation it has given us. I do not really begrudge this church its lighting towers and new microphone. It is just that I cannot get my mind off the bus and the children on the fire escape landing. I cannot forget about Rick.

Such are the two worlds of this and every other American city. In the following pages you will see people from both these worlds. I have recorded them for you so you may see for yourself how far apart these two worlds sometimes are. I do not always know how to bridge the gap. I wait for God to show me some new way.

17

A BURDEN
AND AN
ACHE

———— *MARMALEE* ————

There are many seen and unseen things of beauty in the Inner City. This beauty reveals itself in sometimes strange ways and at unexpected times. It becomes apparent in the music, the customs, and the celebrations of the Inner City. It is found in abundance among the people, their love, their delights, their expectations. Beauty makes life bearable in the Inner City. It is compensation for so much that is ugly, it is light for so much that is dark, it is the future for so much that is past.

Not long ago I sat in the household of Marmalee Dobis on Franklin Street, not far from the church. Marmalee and her family do not attend church, but there is one daughter who sometimes comes to Sunday school. I sat with the Dobis family on this occasion to let them know that I cared about them, that they were wanted and needed in the church, and that we would do everything we could to minister to their family needs.

The household over which Marmalee presides is old, unpainted, and situated in drab surroundings.

18

Marmalee is not married and supports her family on ADC. She is nearly illiterate, inarticulate, afraid of the white world, uncertain of me, afraid of telling me much about herself or her family. Marmalee has had too many interviews with welfare, with people from Operation Pride, social workers, summer youth workers, community councils. She is no longer certain about her house, her community, or her children. She lives precariously in a bewildering world of conflicts.

As best I could I explained to her who I was and why I had come. I do not know now if I said what I wanted to say. Marmalee listened closely but said little in response. As I talked she continued the work she was doing when I came. It was a curious and revealing work. The family wash was the object of her effort, and she entered into this task with the energy and skill born of years of hard work. Marmalee did the family wash in a tub on a stand. A washboard was her instrument of the laundry. She used plenty of detergent and bleach. When she had finished all that was in the tub, she put the pieces in a basket and called two children in the family to hang them out to dry. When this had been done, Marmalee at last sat down on a chair in the center of the room.

The only thing I could think to say that hadn't been said was to ask Marmalee if she would have prayer with me. She looked straight at me with folded hands when she answered, "Yes, I need Jesus to help me in this world." When we prayed, it was a prayer that Jesus would help her in this world. I asked him to help us

19

all. When the prayer was concluded with the amen, she added her own meaningful "Amen, Jesus."

We shook hands as I left, and she smiled. She asked me to come again. As I left the house the clothes that had been hung by the children flapped in the wind, and there was a brilliant contrast between the colors of the wash and the drabness of the unpainted house. Blues, greens, reds, and whites checkered the afternoon air, lighted up the neighborhood, told me much about Marmalee, and waved in the breeze as a thing of beauty in the midst of a drab and somber life.

TONY

Tony is a white boy who does not like to fight. That fact is ominous for Tony's future in the Inner City. As in every community in every part of the world, fighting among schoolchildren is a daily exercise in the Inner City. Whites fight whites, blacks fight blacks, whites fight blacks, girls fight boys. Color, age, and sex have little meaning in fighting. The fighting is often cruel but seldom vicious. I have never known one of these children to be cut by a knife while fighting, although knives are commonly carried and frequently shown. The heart of fighting in the Inner City is with fists, and I think there is some kind of unwritten code of honor about it.

Weakness is the real liability here. The frail children like Tony are seldom protected or assisted. Self-defense is the criterion of existence and acceptance. There is a kind of revulsion against the one who will not fight or defend himself or his group. I do not know that glasses or braces or a cast or sling ever saved an Inner City child from violence or attack. Indeed, it is that child who often becomes the target of attack and punishment.

Yet there comes to me the sight of little Tony being beaten by black boys in the park at dusk. Tony's fair skin and light hair belie his name. He wears glasses, carries books each day, avoids the group, sometimes arrives late to school to avoid fighting, and stays late after school to do the same. All this is to no avail because the exodus of children from school is never-ending, and groups look for fights at all times of the day and night. I have often broken up fights in these parks, but I am careful which ones I break up, and how I intrude in them, for one must not only prevent injury but also preserve the honor of the combatants.

I was not close at hand the afternoon of Tony's siege by a gang of boys, but I could see from a distance that he had the worst of the fight. I could see him writhing on the ground, his glasses lost somewhere in the grass, and boys walking away from him after their victory. What came to my sight that afternoon, and caught at my heart, was the vision of black girls who came to rescue and succor Tony. These girls picked up his books for him, found his glasses, dusted off his clothes, sympathized with him, cursed his tormentors, assured him of their protection the next day, and walked with him the rest of the way to his home. I cannot forget that sight.

Five black girls hovering over one white boy in a park at dusk stands out for me as a rare kind of beauty.

 RUBY

Rudy is a child who sits entranced in the street. Each time I see her on my rounds of the parish, it is in the street. Ruby is four or five years old I would think. The street which makes up her home is bordered by delapidated houses, abandoned cars, stray dogs and children. The street is steep and broken, made up of bricks laid down long ago when it was new like the houses and the people. Ruby is nearly always dirty and ragged. Today she is clad only in underpants. I do not know how long it has been since Ruby has had a bath or has had her hair washed and combed. I sometimes think never. I do not know when she has ever had a good meal or a complete outfit of clothes. Her family is hidden away behind windows that are boarded up and stuffed with papers. I do not know if Ruby has had shots for polio or diptheria or smallpox. Ruby is an urchin.

Today she sits in the middle of the street. I sometimes wonder if she has grown to the pavement in some kind of transplant. Not many cars come along this particular street anymore because of its condition. Not many people live in this block, and that is why Ruby can sit in the street with immunity.

I watch this child Ruby from the sidewalk. I have

spoken to her many times, but she has never spoken in return although she does look up. I have tried to talk to her, to find out some things about her, but she does not respond to me and the neighbors can give me little help. So I watch her today from the vantage point of an elm tree's shade. Ruby is concerned about something she sees in the brick street. She concentrates on it with peculiar, childlike intensity. She picks at it gently, examines it, is engrossed in it. She does not pick it up but rather puts her hands around it as if to protect it. She is oblivious to me and to all the rest of the world. Nothing about her surroundings concerns her in the least.

What Ruby has cupped in her hands today is a white wild daisy growing between the bricks. This daisy is a thing of color and beauty to Ruby—and to me. It has pale blue flecks in each white bloom. Ruby does not destroy it or injure it. She puts her hands around it as if to ward off the dangers of an environment which she has come to know as hostile and destructive. She moves closer to the wild daisy, inching forward on her bare stomach, putting her face next to the flower, smelling its fragrance, feeling the texture of the petals. Ruby will let this flower grow until its life is cast into the oven, for there is something inexorable in Ruby's soul which grasps for beauty. I do not ever want to forget this child Ruby. She, her wild daisy flower, this time and space moment, is a unique and heart-stopping thing of beauty, even, perhaps, a thing of redemption.

——— *SARA* ———

A white woman, a spinster, lives in an old house with a lifetime of gathered things around her. Chairs, boxes, cartons, magazines, books, clothes, a player piano, and photographs from long ago fill each nook and cranny of her home. The smell of moth balls, old newspapers, mice, and dust permeates the hot summer air of her living room. Sara has lived in this house for nearly seventy years. She was born in this house, both her parents died here, and she lives alone with her dust and her mothballs and her memories.

In addition, she lives in this house with her fears. She is afraid of the Inner City in which she dwells, afraid of the people around her, afraid of the children, afraid of the dogs, afraid of all those who fill her circle of life with violence. Many of these people have stolen from her, have entered her house when she was gone, defaced her sidewalks, threatened her, killed the two dogs she bought for protection, broken windows, and thrown refuse on her lawn. She is afraid and stays in her house most of the time, without a telephone or means of defense.

The chair I sit on in Sara's house is nearly in pieces. The chair on which she sits has been nailed and wired. Sara lives on an income totally inadequate for her needs. She has few comforts. Yet, she has faith, and loves people, and forgives her neighbors easily in word and prayer. She is devoted to the church. When she misses morning service we know something unusual has happened. She talks about her life, her profession of nursing,

24

of the people who have visited this house over the years, and of the places she has been. She asks me if I know anyone who might like to buy her old newspapers and magazines, and I tell her I think I know someone.

She offers to fix me a cup of tea. While she prepares it in her small kitchen I examine the photographs, comment on the worth of her books and records and player piano. She is pleased to think that someone believes there are important things in her house. When she returns with our tea, we are seated facing each other once more. The tea is hot and strong. I do not especially care for hot tea but there is something about this cup which gives it flavor. I know it is the flavor of knowing and having communion with this woman.

Serving this cup of tea is important for Sara. It means that there is someone who shares her values and who is interested in her, someone who assures her that she is loved and included. Sara and I drink our tea slowly, chat in an amiable way, each aware of the other in unspoken ways. We look at each other over the cups. Sara smiles. My feeling then is of an exquisite sense of meaning and love for this woman. How much I see in her. I think Sara is beautiful.

 *BENNY*

Benny comes into my office frequently for one reason or another. I do not know specifically why he comes, because he never says. Benny opens the outer door of the

25

church as quietly as he can, comes down the hall with hesitation, and stops at my study door. This door is never closed, and I speak to him in the most friendly manner I know how. Each time Benny comes I ask him to come in and take a chair. Each time he comes he climbs up in the chair which overlooks the yard below. Benny does not say anything to me; he does not speak, asks no questions, answers no questions. He does not tell me his name, where he lives, or why he comes. For a long time I have tried to learn these things about him.

The fact is, I know his name, where he lives, and how old he is, from the people of the settlement next door. The workers of that agency will tell you that Benny is brought to the agency each day during the summer by a white woman, and he is picked up at the end of the day by someone else. They say he is not much of a participant in the agency program but that he is certainly no problem either. Benny sometimes slips away from the agency to cross the parking lot and come to my study. The people at the agency know where he goes and we have an understanding about that.

I am glad that Benny comes. He is a mixture of white and black and perhaps Indian. He is a handsome, compelling, mystical boy. Whether he is the shadow of some act of teen-age passion, is adopted, or just a member of some normal family life we do not exactly know. All I know is that Benny is a boy of our future civilization, a blending of the blood and genes of several races, carrying within him the best, and very possibly the worst, of all the races he represents.

26

When I first saw Benny at the door of the church he had a tag around his neck. This tag had been placed there by one of the workers at the agency. This worker is a college student, working at the agency as a summer volunteer. She is attractive and high-spirited, caught up in the power of this human rights effort, optimistic about her work, and certain that that work will bear fruit during her summer term. She does not know yet, in the inner part of her, that she can grow old in this work without seeing any permanent, tangible change in the lives of all the Bennys she knows. Customs, family habits, cultural traditions, all make these children, indeed make all of us, what we are, and we are not made or unmade in one summer or even two or more. We do not yet know how many summers it will take to unmake some things.

This worker, like I, sees Benny and tries to communicate with him—but to little avail. She loves him in her vital feminine way, is affectionate with him, and tries to involve him. But he is aloof, quite content to live within himself. She remains steadfast, nevertheless, and tells us in the evaluation sessions that she thinks Benny is making progress.

I doubt it. I do not know what she means exactly by progress, but I do not think Benny is much nearer to being a member of the order of things, or much more aware of that order, than he ever was. I think that at eight or so, which is his age, Benny is pretty much who he will be, and that no social agency or clergyman will cause him to "progress." Benny, whoever he is, from wherever he comes, is a product of our society and we will hear more from him, pay some penalties and reap some rewards, because of him.

In the meantime, he watches me and I him, and there is a communion between us which I do not understand, but which I hope Benny does.

ERNESTINE

Ernestine is a deformed and ugly child. She drools at the mouth because she has no control over her swallowing. She is eight and weighs something like twenty-five pounds. She is fed through a tube which is inserted in her throat. She fouls her undergarments and is diapered like a baby. The neighbors cannot bear to look at her. The other children in the family are accustomed to her but do little for her because her parents have not wanted them to be burdened by her. Ernestine suffered cruel brain damage at birth, the doctors say. They also have said that with early treatment and therapy Ernestine might have been helped. She is now past helping, and the doctors advise the parents to have Ernestine placed in an institution.

I think perhaps they are right, and yet I know her parents love her and I am not so sure that putting her in an institution is the thing to do. It is true that she would get the medical care that she does not receive at home. Ernestine's parents are very poor and uneducated and unacquainted with many simple laws of health and hygiene. Yet every night of the week Ernestine's father comes home from work, chews food from the table, and forces it from his mouth into the tube and down the throat of Ernestine. This child lives on food chewed by her father. In an institution this would be done by a machine. It would be more sanitary and probably more effective.

But who is to say that it is not being done under expert care and supervision now? At least the doctors say Ernestine will never starve to death. Ernestine will die sometime before she is much older, I suspect, but in the meantime I have that image of a father in dirty jeans and T-shirt with grimy hands from work, holding a deformed child in his arms, hugging that child close to him, gently pushing the substance of life down a tube, holding and nourishing a frail bit of unlovely life which is made somehow lovely by his love. This is a picture that haunts me, a picture that taken in its entirety becomes a thing of almost ethereal beauty.

LEO ANDERSEN

Leo Andersen stands before a hostile crowd of blacks on the Near North Side. Patrolman Andersen has been called to break up a gang forming on a grocery store parking lot. This lot has been the scene of many a fight and riot, and from it groups have gone out to loot, burn, snipe, and destroy.

Leo Andersen wishes he were somewhere else. He hates the Inner City, not so much because it is black, but because the ways of the people here, both black and white, are unfathomably foreign to him. He has been here many times before. He has been shot at, slandered, cursed, criticized, and manhandled. He has broken up fights, protected store owners from hoodlums, protected hoodlums from store owners, directed traffic while blacks burned down their own homes, and taken abuse from the people he protected.

Leo is a good man by all normal standards. He is forty years old and has been a policeman for twelve years. He makes about $6,000 per year but retirement and a lot of other things come out of his check. Leo works long hours and takes his responsibility as a police officer seriously. His wife tells me he takes it too seriously. Leo is Catholic, enjoys beer and movies, never cared much for reading, barely got through high school. He will tell you that there are a good many things in this life that he does not understand, and the one of those things he understands the least is these people who burn down their own homes. Not in a thousand years, he says, will he understand why they do what they do, why they live the way they live, why they seem so bent on destroying themselves and others. Leo has thought many times about leaving the force and getting a quiet job on a farm. Twice already he has asked for a transfer away from this beat. Yet while he is here he serves the best he knows how.

Leo is called today to break up a fight. A crowd has gathered on the parking lot, the weather is hot and everyone is out-of-doors. There is laughter, hooting, and a general tense feeling in the air. When Leo arrives he is greeted with obscenities and threats, and there is shoving and pushing as he makes his way toward the center of the disturbance. He notes the number of people, the ages, the number of whites, the number of women, the mood which is always capable of exploding into chaos. Leo steps without hesitation toward three men who are drunk and fighting. No one bars his way, but he can feel the hostility and can hear the threats and curses. Leo does not put his hands on the men fighting, but in a voice filled with authority and force he orders the men to break up the fight or he will arrest them. Slowly the three men respond to Leo's demands, but the crowd does not give way. They dare Leo to touch one of the three men. Members of the crowd warn Leo that they will kill him if he uses his club. Leo does not take notice of these threats and he is not about to back down. He is prepared to enforce the law and prepared to suffer the consequences. It has all happened before in Leo's career. A fight, police, a crowd, a riot. Leo wishes he were on the farm.

At that moment, when the situation seems to be moving out of Leo's control, at that moment when he knows it might all come to violence, a Catholic priest steps forward into the crowd. Father Krause is a veteran of this street, his church and settlement house being not far away. Father Krause is an old man, I think, but you can never be sure in this way of life. He is grim and probably frightened himself, but he knows his role, and he knows these people, and he does his thing. He says, in a voice that rattles the rats in the sewer, "Now that's just about

31

enough! This officer is here to help this community and we must do what he says or we will all suffer. Break up this damn foolishness and go back where you all belong." The veins stand out in his neck to give credence to his decree.

In some way which I do not understand, this man, with his voice and bearing, his courage and audacity, is adequate to harness the power of the crowd. There is murmuring, laughter, derision, and shouted threats of retaliation, but no violence. Leo, with a relief which he knows everyone recognizes, takes up conversation with those who stand close to him. Father Krause and Leo do not speak but there is an understanding. Father Krause goes back to his settlement house, Leo back to his cruiser, and the crowd goes back into the stores and bars and back alleys. In that moment there has been a coming together of two vital kinds of authority in our society, the patient but firm authority of the law and the godly authority of a priest. It has been sufficient to harness the power of a mob. That authority which neither Leo nor Father Krause would be quite able to define is a very special thing in the Inner City, and it makes me thankful for its way among violent men.

——— *ARCHER* ———

Many of the relationships I have with people in the Inner City begin with telephone calls. These calls come at all hours of the day and night; they come from phone booths, jail, court, and the mission, and they are always from people who have some special need.

One call came late at night from a booth on Hamilton Street. The caller identified himself by name (this is not always the case), asked if I could come down to a certain address, and said he would wait for me. He had a very important matter to talk over with me, he said. In all honesty I must say that I use some caution in where I go at night and who I meet. Strange things happen to the unwary in the Inner City. Yet the voice was urgent, and because there was a note of honesty in it, I promised to meet him on schedule.

I strapped myself in the VW and drove over rough streets to 30th and Hamilton on the east side of this parish. The caller was waiting for me by the phone booth as he had promised. We introduced ourselves and I invited him into the VW. He asked me to drive him to a certain address on Hamilton. On the way he apologized for asking me to come so late at night, but he explained that the matter was urgent and he did not know who to go to for help except the pastor whose name he had seen on the bulletin board outside the church.

The man sitting beside me was middle-aged, black, and tired-looking. He explained that he had driven up from Dallas without stopping for rest and that he had had little rest or food since arriving in Omaha. Most of all, he wanted to show me something. "It's the best thing that ever happened to me, Reverend," he said. With an excitement I could feel he directed me to a shop on Hamilton Street where we parked and got out of the

33

VW. He opened the door to what I could easily see was a run-down junk shop. Inside, once the lights were turned on, there was to be seen a jungle of broken furniture, old television sets, beds, boards, dishes, trunks, rope, wire, clothes, and toys. Debris and clutter were everywhere.

Inside the shop this new-found companion introduced me to a woman he identified as his mother. She was a patient-looking woman, wise in the ways of white people, apprehensive yet confident. When the mother and I had spoken and passed the barrier of being strangers, she explained that she had had twenty children and that this son was the best of the family, always went to church (in fact he had introduced himself as a minister), was honest and law-abiding. The mother seemed anxious for me to know this. Together they explained that this store was the property of the mother, who had operated it for many years. What she wanted now was to go back to Texas to be with her people. She wanted this son to have the shop in order to support himself in his itinerant ministry and to support his family. She commented that she would be proud to have her son as a businessman in the community. "We ain't never had none of our folks in business before," she said.

The mother wanted to sell the shop to her son for $90. The Small Business Administration would provide $45 of the purchase price if mother and son could match that amount. Was there any way I could help to get them the money? The good Lord knows we will pay you back every cent, they promised.

Truth to tell, I did not know where to get $45. But I

have learned something about the Inner City. It is that sometimes you go on faith, and that truth is vitally important in establishing relationships with people who live there. I told Archer and his mother that I would do what I could to get them the money. For the next two days Archer and I made our rounds talking to people who might help. In making the rounds I also came to know Archer.

The farm on which he was born was red clay and bone dry. The corn died year after year and the young pigs always had to be sold before they were half grown. The children were born one every year, lived on the cutting edge of starvation, seldom attended school, roamed the countryside in search for rabbits, fruit, fish, and anything else that was edible. Archer never saw money until he was a teen-ager. His father was in and out of jails for stealing (food, Archer thinks). Whites abused the family and saw five of the children die of sickness rooted in malnutrition. When Archer left home, never to return, he was thirteen and ready for a man's responsibility in the fields at $1.50 per day. Working in the fields and hauling garbage was all that Archer had ever learned to do. Even now I can catch only a glimpse of the unbelievable excitement that gripped him at the prospect of owning a store. I can still remember how his hands trembled at the thought.

We raised the money. When he had it all, his joy was past description. His car had been sold to buy food for his family. His clothes were past mending and his shoes were ripped at the seams. He had little to remember of

35

the past and a precarious future before him. But Archer
Williams was now a businessman and neither past nor
future mattered much, only this delectable present.

Archer opens the store each day at about 8:00 A.M. He
does a good business and puts a little money in the bank.
His children are in school, he sometimes preaches at a
nearby holiness church, and I browse around the store
occasionally to see how things are with him. It is still run-
down and cluttered, but Archer presides over it with a
spirit that makes me humble. I buy something from him
now and then, and not long ago he gave me a trunk
which I had hoped to buy. I wanted to pay for it but he
insisted I take it. The money we borrowed is all paid
back, and Archer repays the society which gave him the
chance he wanted with responsible citizenship. He wants
it to be this way. A better future for his children than he
ever know in the past. Hope lives on in the Inner City.

──────── *STELLA* ────────

On another occasion the call came from an adult proba-
tion officer. He was calling for Stella. In a drunken stupor
she had set fire to her hotel room, and the fire had
burned out the whole hotel and three people had died.
Stella was charged with manslaughter and wanted to see
a minister. She was nineteen, away from the reservation
for the first time, and married to a white man who had
disappeared. Under those circumstances Stella had too
many strikes against her. First, she was an Indian, sec-

36

ondly she was a transient, and third she had no money. Stella was as good as convicted before she ever saw the inside of the jail.

With as much dispatch as possible, we made arrangements to have people from the Indian community in Omaha visit her in jail. There we found her hysterical and nearly incoherent. Could we get her a lawyer, she wanted to know. Could we find her husband? Would we talk to the county attorney? Could we raise $5,000 bond? Could we get the charge reduced? What would happen to her? Could we get her a coat? "Oh God," she wailed, "those poor people who burned up."

A lawyer? Bond? Reduced charge? For a transient Indian? Getting the coat was about all society was prepared to concede. Goodwill will always help with that. We did find her husband through Indian contacts. When I talked to the county attorney's office, all they would say was that they had no idea when her preliminary hearing would be, who the prosecutor would be, or what penalty they would press for. I talked to the public defender's office in the same courthouse. The fire which Stella had caused had raged only three days before. Pictures of Stella had appeared on the front page of the newspaper for two days, she was shown hysterical before the hotel on television, pictures of the three dead victims were familiar to nearly every citizen of Omaha, and the public defender asked me, "Stella who?"

The truth is, in this society Stella is nobody. She is a drag, an unfortunate, a headache, a public burden. Her trial will be held soon, she will be convicted like so many others before her, there will be no witnesses for the defense, the defender will do his public duty, Stella will be incarcerated without appeal or hope of early parole, and the case will be closed forever.

I talked to an attorney whom I thought might give me some advice about Stella and his only question was, "Do you have any money to pay for my services?" Such is justice in the Inner City. It is this kind of justice which renders me dumb when people ask why the poor are so hostile to the police and to the law. My only answer can be that in our society justice works according to the amount of money which is available. I cannot buy much of the law for people of the Inner City. If I had more money I could buy more of it. It is bought every day in these courts. I would add that anyone who wants to know the source of this hostility and mistrust needs to stand for one day in police court or any other court as people of the Inner City are brought in for hearings, appeals, and trials, and his wonderings will be stilled. Talk to Stella in prison. She has something to say about it all.

LUCILLE

A telephone call which has a familiar note comes this morning from Lucille in a downtown cafe. Would it be possible for me to lend her eight dollars? She needs it to buy some school things for her children, supplies, lunches, a pair of overshoes at the Salvation Army store.

She will pay me back the first of the month. Could I come down to Sixteenth Street with the money?

Today I cannot give her the money. Last week I gave some to Marian and tomorrow it will be to Davie or Joan. It may be for the children again, or a funeral, or a delivery of fuel oil, or a lawyer for a son in trouble. The needs change, the names of the people change, but the request is always the same. Could I lend them five dollars until the first of the week, or ten dollars until Friday, or twenty dollars until ADC comes in? It may be coal in the winter or ice in the summer, since coal and ice are still basic ingredients in the Inner City.

I really believe that Lucille wants this money today to pay off some debt for her husband. It may be to a loan shark or for some gambling debt, but I know it will not be for Lucille herself. I have met Lucille many times in my ministry in the Inner City. She is a woman usually big with child. I do not know how many children she does have exactly. They are all born in her own home and I do not even know if they are registered with the state. She supports her family with piecemeal work, charity and begging. Her husband works a little now and then but spends most of his time, and all of his money, on gambling and women.

I have tried to get Lucille to do several things. I have asked her to undergo sterilization, separate herself from her commonlaw husband, apply for ADC, and move into a different neighborhood. Lucille will do none of these things. They are against her principles, she says. She is wise in a rather strange way, and does possess a very unusual kind of loyalty. She cannot betray what she thinks is her position in life as a woman and mother by undergoing sterilization, she feels loyalty to the man who keeps her pregnant, and she thinks that moving from the neighborhood where she was born and where she lives would be to betray the people who live there. I remind Lucille that this way of life is nearly criminal for herself and her children. In those moments when I lose my patience with her I tell her that she has no right to expect other people to give her money or clothes or to pay her rent. On occasion I have told her that I will have nothing more to do with her and that I will not help her anymore. Lucille knows I will do nothing of the sort. While she knows that I will not give her money or take a child to the hospital if that is not possible for me at any given time, she does know that I will not abandon her or cease to love her and her children. She knows very well she has me there. We both know I will do what I can.

I will give the money when I have it. Five dollars here, ten dollars there, twenty dollars somewhere else. Sometimes my giving narrows down to giving a cup of coffee or to a warm breakfast for a transient. I do not know how much money I have given away in the Inner City. Giving it is very likely wrong, of course, because I do not always have control over how it is finally spent. Besides, begging as such is no longer really necessary in this society. Yet, it is sometimes the most dignified way, and nearly always the fastest way, for some sick person to get medicine, or a hungry person to be fed, or a wanderer to get a room for the night. It is not always possible

40

to decide whether the need is strictly legitimate. Sometimes I take their word for it, and because I trust them they trust me in return. I am seldom betrayed.

Lucille is my friend. When she calls again, or when I see her downtown, she will have some word of hope for me about her tomorrow.

CONNIE

Connie is a member of a church-related youth group in the Inner City. She attends the group regularly Tuesday evenings. She has never held office but does not seem bothered by this and is a part of most activities of the group. She is sixteen years old, white, moderately attractive as a teen-ager with a good figure. She dresses well, has a certain natural poise, seems well-adjusted, and laughs easily. Connie is the oldest of seven children. Her father is unemployed and probably an alcoholic. Her mother works part time in a cafe, draws welfare assistance, and pays little attention to her children. I have often been in Connie's home and it is always a struggle. The place is a pile of filth and smells of cats and sour milk. The other children in Connie's family have never been to Sunday school although Connie does try to get them to come. They have attended some of the activities of the agency next door.

Connie is the real mother to these children. She does not seem to be able to untangle the problems of the home, but she does provide what stability and care there is. She prepares most of the meals, tries to keep the children clean and decently dressed, and watches over them as best she can. Four of the children attend public school, but they have a poor attendance record. Community and school workers often come to the home to look for the children when they are absent. These community workers have tried to do something about the situation in the home, but the city and county authorities know it is no worse than a hundred other homes. They have sometimes threatened to place the children in foster homes or an institution, but this is mostly threat. There are too many homes like this in the community to make it easy to start and stop the process of taking children away from homes.

Connie is not a good student herself, but she is not always a bad one, either. Her grades are average in most subjects but she gets good marks in things like cooperation, attitude, and deportment. Some of her teachers tell me they like Connie very much and try to help her in whatever way they can. While her attendance record is poor, there is no attempt to declare her a truant or delinquent. She has been in Youth Bureau a number of times but has never been committed to a correctional institution. Each time she is sent home with a warning, and I am notified that she has been released.

Connie, at the age of sixteen, is an experienced prostitute. Her parents know it, school officials know it, Youth Bureau workers know it but ignore it. The reason

Connie continues to involve herself in prostitution with immunity is that she is shrewd about it. She is careful about the men with whom she has sexual relations. She is careful about the places where she meets these men. She is especially careful about when these relations take place. Connie tells me that she is intimate with not more than five men altogether, that they are all men of means, that she is available only on weekends and school holidays, and that sexual relations are always held in cars, never in homes or motels. In this way Connie escapes scrutiny by neighbors and the law, does not get involved with dangerous characters, does not let her sexual practices interfere with her schoolwork, and does not let them take her away from the other children in the family. Connie says the number of times she has intercourse on any given weekend will depend on how much money the men have. She never tells me what she earns. She buys her own contraceptives, a practice carefully taught and followed among many Inner City girls.

With the money Connie earns she supports her family with food and other necessities, tries to have clothes for herself, probably gives much of it to her parents, does give some of it to other people who want to borrow from her, and spends a little on herself for simple pleasures. She does not date boys her own age.

Connie is not an oversexed girl in any sense of the word. She does not entice men and is not especially aware of her own sexuality. She is just a young girl who has learned that money is important for herself and her

43

family, and that she has something which men want and are willing to pay money for. I doubt that she receives any satisfaction from the sex act. She tells me she thinks she first had sexual relations with a man when she was eleven or twelve. She does not use vulgar language, does not smoke, does not take part in suggestive acts or tell smutty stories. She is not an outwardly immoral person as we think of that term. She is a teen-ager of the Inner City, and there are girls like her everywhere in this parish.

I talk endlessly with Connie. I have talked to her teachers, her mother, her social worker, and with county officials. They all agree that she probably ought to be put in a foster home. They can put her there or leave her where she is. They prefer to do the latter. I have mixed feelings about that, but I think I agree with their decision. I could apply enough pressure to have Connie committed. I am not sure I have this right, and it might very well be a mistake for me to say that the intent of such action would be to reform Connie by giving her a new environment. I know where she would be sent, and I have no confidence that this school for girls would be an improvement over the environment where she is now.

I talk to her about her life, about ideals and the future, about marriage and raising a family, about the danger of what she is now doing. She listens intently to me and sometimes laughs at me and says she wants all the things I describe. When I suggest that her present way of life might very well jeopardize her whole future, she says

44

she doesn't think it will and sees no reason why it should. When I tell her that I can find another place for her to live, another city, another family, another set of friends, another school, she replies very firmly that she has no wish to leave her family or her community. On occasion when I have asked her to give up her life of promiscuity she has replied that she could give it up anytime she wanted to, and that sometime she will, but not now. I have prayed with her on occasion, but she does not close her eyes or make any comment. She respects me, I think, but has not let me discourage her pattern of life, which may well destroy her whole life and future, her ability to be a mother and wife and an effective member of society. I must confess that I used to be more certain about this than I am now. Strange things happen in the Inner City. I continue to be her friend, and to pray for her, and to let her know I do not approve of what she does. I attempt to keep open her place in the youth group so that she will be included and feel accepted.

I do not know how it will all come out. For the Inner City abounds in Connies, and in the men who make the Connies what they are, and I cannot undo that, either here or elsewhere. Only a massive social restructuring of family life, education, housing, social welfare, and counseling can do that. We are nowhere near that kind of program today, here or anywhere else in American society. For a long time to come we will be required to minister in what ways we can to all the Connies of this world.

—————— *JAMIE LEE* ——————

Jamie Lee was shot to death not far from one of the churches in this parish. I did not know Jamie in life but I met him in death. On that day of his funeral I discovered him to be a boy of fine features, filled with that young and energetic power which gives all youth of the world today such promise. In life Jamie Lee was said to be restless and driven by some inward impatience. In death he was lost forever to the promise of youth.

In the weeks after Jamie's death I got to know him through his family and his friends. He was seventeen when he died, one of many children, a descendant of slaves, fatherless, motherless, a ward of the court and of relatives. Jamie was a carrier of burdens, having heaped up in him the misery and anger of a heritage of oppression. He lived in a city which has always kept its blacks effectively in their place. Jamie knew from earliest childhood which streets were safe for black children and which ones were dangerous for them. He knew from painful experience which parks and swimming pools and theaters were available to him. He gathered in the lore of the black community and learned where he could be and could not be after 10:00 at night. From experience he learned quickly about police. He knew which ones he could trust and which ones were the enemy. Jamie developed, with his contemporaries in the ghetto, that sharp and sensitive sense of what it takes to stay alive on these streets. Jamie Lee reached for manhood in an age and in a society which tried to thwart that manhood be-

46

cause it was black. Jamie and society together paid a terrible price for that thwarting.

One hot summer night Jamie and a friend stole a car. They drove the car west off Thirtieth Street. They raced away from a patrolman who tried to stop them, running at least two red lights, moving through a congested section of the city at high speed. We have Jamie's friend as a witness to what Jamie did and said and felt in those moments of the chase. Lonnie tells the story simply and clearly.

"Jamie only meant to use the car to get to his grandmother's. That woman was the only family Jamie had. He had this trouble with the principal at school, you know, and he didn't know what to do. He thought they was goin' to expel him, and he had to talk to somebody. Seems like nobody would ever listen to Jamie. I told him not to take the car, but he had to get there and back the same night so as not to be late to school the next day. The car was just sittin' there with the keys in it, and Jamie said they wouldn't even miss it."

Lonnie twisted his hands in his lap. "When the police spotted the car I told Jamie we ought to stop, that they would shoot us if we didn't. But Jamie said they wouldn't shoot just for a stolen car, and he really thought they wouldn't. Just before he was hit he said he hoped his grandmother would be waitin' up for him. Jamie was awful scared. Seems like he was always scared and doin' the wrong things when he wanted to do the right thing. Why couldn't somebody ever try to help him?" Lonnie

47

stared straight ahead and I saw the anguish of his soul as he asked the question of all of us in this city.

I cannot know all the things that went through Jamie's mind in those fleeting moments before his death. To Lonnie's testimony must be added the witness of Jamie's grandmother and Jamie's friends in the neighborhood. We can be sure that Jamie would have remembered in the moments of that pursuit what police and courts and white witnesses and white lawyers mean to a black boy in this city. Whatever Jamie meant to do, the fact remains that he shot the car straight ahead at high speed. With a patrol car in pursuit, red light flashing, siren wailing, Jamie sped north past the church. He did not get far before he was hit by a shotgun blast from the patrol car. He died on the way to County Hospital, his young life and all the unfulfilled promises, forming red blotches on the covering sheet.

There was rioting in Omaha after Jamie's death. Negroes wailed for him and for themselves. They lashed out in violence and the white community reacted in violence. When it was all over, both blacks and whites assessed the meaning of Jamie's death. He cannot know that when I visited the police department, the city library, the county attorney's office, a few months after his death, their quizzical reply was always the same, "Who was Jamie Lee?" All agreed that his death should not have happened. The court of inquiry exonerated the police officer. Whatever Jamie's death meant in its entirety, it meant that no one understood it. Jamie did not die from persecution, as a victim of a riot, or of any conspiracy or program of hate. His death was not caused specifically by white racism, or black nationalism, or racial conflict. He died nearly alone in this city, and his death cannot be proved to be the result of any one of these things.

Yet, in my more profound moments, I know his death was the result of all these things. What grief did whites feel at the death of this young man, whatever his race? What did the police feel beyond having done their duty? What response did a city make about the death of a young man who had neither father nor mother? Did Christians share the hurt with outrage? Only by probing deeply into these responses is it possible for us to avert the death of other Jamies.

At his funeral we saw Jamie Lee more clearly, I think. In a sense he came into focus for those of us who had seen him only dimly before. His relatives and friends from school were there. In attendance were representatives of the whole community: educators, city officials, and spectators. They all came to the ritual of putting away forever one young black man who always seemed to do the wrong thing when he really wanted to do the right thing. Jamie's minister spoke kind and compassionate words with a special eye to all the young people there. He cautioned against violence and retaliation. He asked that both blacks and whites seek answers to common problems within their own hearts and feelings.

At Jamie's funeral we all sat dumb and stricken. What can a white man say or do in a black church, at the funeral of a black youth who has been shot by a white policeman? I sat and knew deep in my soul that I owed Jamie Lee something. I did not know then, nor do I know now, what it was that I owed him. I am trying to discover what it was, exactly, so that I can give it, or share it with someone in Jamie's name, so that I, and he, will have given something.

———— JOE THE INDIAN ————

One evening, not so long ago, I sat for a while in the house of Joe the Indian. Joe is a dying man, although he and I have never spoken of it. The records we have at the church say his name is Joseph Lewis. The telephone directory lists him as J. W. Lewis. At his place of work they call him Joe. In the records at the reservation, where he draws an allowance from the government for use of his tribal lands, he is listed as Bear That Never Thirsts. I do not know the Santee symbols for that name. I sometimes wonder if that name might have been given him by a mother who hoped, thereby, to ward off an evil spirit that plagued her own household. I do know the name does not fit Joe, because in reality he is the bear whose thirst is never quenched.

Bear That Never Thirsts is dying of cirrhosis of the liver, brought on by a lifetime of drinking. Joe is not a drunk by normal standards. He does not stagger on the street, is never picked up for vagrancy, does not brawl or even lose time from work. Joe has worked in the same appliance factory for over seven years, and the only time he has had off from work has been to visit the reservation or to enter the hospital. Joe has spent a great deal of time in the hospital, as a matter of fact. Periodically he becomes ill from drinking and enters the hospital for treatment. County officials know they could commit Joe to the State Hospital as a confirmed alcoholic, but all of us agree that he would die there, as if in a prison. Joe remains in the hospital until his strength is built up, and then he is released to his work and his drinking.

Joe works eight hours every day. He brings his lunch to work in a brown paper sack. It is usually a bag of corn chips and a piece of pastry. He buys coffee in the hall canteen. He does not sit in the cafeteria with the other workers. Joe eats alone in the workroom. When his shift is out at 4:30 he leaves with the crew, and, as been his custom for so many years that no one can remember how long it has been, he stops at a tavern some blocks from the factory. He drinks about $3.00 worth of liquor. When he goes home at 6:00 he eats some bread and meat, or opens a can of soup, or perhaps finishes something he began the day before. After supper he watches television and drinks. Normally, he falls asleep in the chair. Sometimes he gets up during the night and goes to bed, but sometimes he sleeps all night in the chair and gets up from that chair the next morning to go to work. His breakfast is usually oatmeal or cold cereal and coffee. He leaves for work at 6:30 and walks to work whatever the weather. Such is the daily life of Bear Who Never Thirsts.

51

It is said in the neighborhood that Joe has children living in the community, but no one seems to be able to point them out. Some say he left his wife on the reservation when he came to Omaha. Others say he never married. Some say he has had several wives. I do not know. Here it does not really matter.

Joe came to the church once, with some of his friends. It was a community meeting of Indians, and I suppose the prospect of a warm meal, at a time when the weather was very cold, had some appeal for him. He sat with his friends and ate his supper. I became acquainted with Joe on that occasion, and even though he only answered questions put to him, I think he felt some pleasure in being noticed and included. I invited him back to church, but he never came. I am not sure that there is really anything at the church which meets Joe's needs, except a group of people who care. Joe says he is not interested in becoming a Christian. He seems very far away from anything I might say from the pulpit, except that God loves his children whoever and wherever they are. It may very well be that Joe needs his ancient tribal religion. There are a great many members of the Indian community here, who practice that religion as best they can in an urban environment. Peyote is available here and used extensively among the Indians. Christians have tried very hard to destroy a faith which might well be the only religious faith Joe feels and can understand. I do not think we are justified in that.

I often visit with Joe in this house. It vibrates anxiously as the trains roar by only fifty yards away. The roaring

and shaking keep Joe's television out of focus. He bangs
on it periodically to keep it working. I always come after
supper and he is usually drinking. He does not interrupt
his drinking, and offers to share his bottle with me. He
speaks briefly, now and then, of the reservation and his
boyhood, of some of the things he remembers so well
from the past. He talks of the horses and the cattle kills
and of trips down the Missouri River. He speaks of his
mother especially, and of her death in a great blizzard.
Joe also talks about his work record at the factory. He is
inordinately proud of that record, as I can understand,
and says he has saved some of his money. Somehow, in
listening to Joe talk and reminisce about his past, I get
the feeling that what happened in the space of time between the young boy who was Bear Who Never Thirsts
and the old man we call Joe might account for a great
many things in the lives of all the Indians in our American society.

There are many Indians in the Inner City. They are
more poor and alienated than any other minority group.
They are alienated from their own people. There is little
communication with the white community and as little
communication within the Indian community. In so
many deep-seated ways, most of the Indians have never
left the reservation. They know that the reservation, for
all its lack of opportunity, employment, and education,
still provides a security which can never be found in the
white man's world of tall buildings and noisy streets. Indians are seldom at home away from the reservation, and
in the city most of their dreaming has to do with a return

53

to that reservation. Indians live in housing which the Negroes have vacated. They live mutely, in poverty and neglect. The heritage of the Indian has not been one of complaint, and I think this works destructively against them today. They live and die, work and suffer, in a silence which kills them.

This man whom I call Joe, this man whom I watch dying, is really four people. He is Bear That Never Thirsts, a descendant of what he knows is a rich and powerful tradition. He is J. W. Lewis to the telephone company, a sophisticated but forlorn name that means nothing. The church lists him as Joseph, which is some better, at least giving him the dignity of a full name, whether it is really his name or not. At work he is Joe, and he might as well be something else, for he does not identify with that name. He knows himself to be something other than Joe. I doubt that he can define what that something is, but Bear That Never Thirsts is ever with him. Perhaps he drinks to drown out what he knows he is, and can never be. Perhaps he drinks to drown out what he is, but does not want to be.

Sometime soon Bear That Never Thirsts will die. If he lists a friend or relative on the hospital record, they will be notified and arrangements will be made to return him to the reservation for burial. Otherwise the county will bury him in the pauper's section of the cemetery, and after a while there will be no trace of Bear That Never Thirsts, of J. W. Lewis, of Joseph Lewis, or of Joe.

There comes to me, at different times when I talk to Joe, or to his Indian friends, or to any Indian who enters my life and ministry in the Inner City, a remarkably revealing prayer of the Chippewas. This prayer about the lake speaks of the transition through which the American Indian now moves in our society. What will become of the Indian in this kind of society, urban and industrial? For that matter what will become of all the poor and disenfranchised in this society? What will be come of any of us? That prayer implores:

> "O Great Spirit! Thou hast made this lake;
> Thou hast also created us as Thy children;
> Thou art able to make this water calm
> Until we have safely passed over."

———— *JOHN PACEK* ————

John Pacek is the owner and proprietor of a dry goods store in the Inner City. His particular neighborhood is one of the better ones in the community. The building which houses his store is old but well kept. The merchandise he stocks and sells covers the basic necessities of the people in the neighborhood. He deals in clothing: men's shirts and pants, ties, socks, underwear; some dresses, hose, blouses, underthings for women; children's clothing, yard goods, some household wares, and an assortment of things which people have asked for over the years, form his inventory. John Pacek knows the needs of the people of this community very well, and he has learned what to stock, and what not to stock, over the years. He has owned this store on this corner for nearly forty years. It has made him a good living. It has put his children through school, provided him a comfortable home, a new car occasionally, enough money for his old age, and some security for the time when the store will pass to other owners.

John Pacek came to this country when he was nineteen years old. He came alone and penniless. He worked for the New York Street Department, as night custodian in a grocery store, and in a garage as clean-up man. When he was twenty-one he emigrated to Council Bluffs, Iowa, in answer to an ad about employment in the Union Pacific Railroad shops. The next year he began working as a clerk in a grocery store in Omaha. Thirteen years later, when the store owner died, John Pacek raised enough money to buy the store. It is that store which John operates now in the Inner City. When the store was his at last, John Pacek married, managed the store frugally, and became a respected citizen and businessman in his white, Bohemian, Presbyterian community.

In 1949 Negroes began moving into the neighborhood around John Pacek's store. Most of these blacks came from the Omaha ghetto, although some of them had only recently arrived from the south. Businessmen and property owners were alarmed by this movement of the Negroes. The fear was for property values, for the safety of women and children, and for the appearance of the community. For a time these problems were held in abeyance, for few blacks patronized white stores. But slowly, as blacks continued to move into the neighborhood, there began a continuous stream of Negroes into all stores, including John Pacek's. These blacks had money, and John made profits selling to them, but he had difficulty accepting them. He resented their aggressiveness, their lack of respect for white people and white ways, and the endless number of them. He waited on them, but let them know that he was not happy with them, and that he did not care whether they traded with him or not. He did not bother to stock items which the blacks especially asked for, and he told the children to mind their manners.

In 1952, in agreement with other businessmen in the neighborhood, John Pacek posted a sign in his store window which read, "No Colored Allowed." For a time this blunt sign succeeded in keeping the blacks away. But, these Negroes taught John Pacek a hard and lasting lesson. He began to hurt economically. Many of the white residents of the community were moving away as the blacks moved in. Many of those who stayed refused to enter stores which sold to blacks. John Pacek began to see that these blacks, for all their ways and lack of respect for white people, were the long-range security for his business. In 1954, without any agreement with other businessmen, John removed the "No Colored Allowed" sign from his store window. He could not depend on white people for his livelihood; now he must depend on blacks. Within a matter of days his business with blacks was restored.

John Pacek discovered that he could raise his prices because Negroes were not always familiar with competitive buying. He also discovered that he could buy inferior merchandise and resell it in the store for a 100 percent markup. He found that he could sometimes sell a child a dollar's worth of goods when the child only wanted ten cents' worth. Now and then he accepted credit, and discovered that when the family did not keep its purchase slips, it usually accepted the bill he submitted at the end of the month. John Pacek prospered.

The neighborhood around John's store is nearly all black now, except for a few white families that have stayed. John is seventy years old, and would like to sell the store. He once said he would never sell the store to a black, but now no white man wants it. John would sell the store to a black now, but he cannot find a buyer. The merchandise is still marked up, but the Negroes know all about that now. The quality is of varying standards. John is afraid for the safety of his store. He cannot get white counter help and will not hire black help. He and his store have suffered. Windows have been broken, merchandise stolen, and he has been taunted and cursed. John Pacek is old and tired, and the stress of the business wears on him like iron. He would like to retire to his garden.

John feels strongly about private enterprise. He cashes ADC checks, and knows how many people in the community live off welfare, or charity, as he calls it. John says very emotionally that welfare is wrong. He can tell you how hard he worked, how he saved, what he did to get ahead in the world. He does not feel he owes any man a thing, or that the government does, either. Hard work is the key to life, John Pacek says. "What I did, they can too," he adds.

John has never been in the home of a Negro, that he can remember. He has never had a Negro in his home, except as deliveryman. He does not live in the community surrounding his store. He has no special friends who are black. He has never, within memory, attended a meeting of the school board, the PTA, the Community Council, or the Neighborhood Block club. John Pacek says he does not understand Negroes.

On one occasion, as he explained the reasons for his hard-won success in life, I said to him, "John, never in your life have you lost a job, or been turned down for one, because of the color of your skin. As hard as you have worked, you have never tried to buy a house, or board a streetcar, or eat in a restaurant, or sit on a park bench, or attend a church, and had someone say to you, "You can't do that because you are black!" You have never had anyone pass laws against you, or run you out of town, or try to lynch you, or insult your children, or try to keep you in one part of town. Never in your life, John, has your *color* been the difference between life and death."

John looks at me as from an unfathomable distance and replies, "I don't believe color makes that much difference to anyone. It has never made any difference to me."

———— *ADA* ————

On a cold, blustery afternoon just before Thanksgiving, a member of one of the parish churches asks me if I will take her to University Hospital. Ada Thomas is well past sixty years of age, a widow, poor, nearly blind. She will enter University Hospital for free medical care. I bundle her in a wool comforter wrapped around her sweater and coat. Ada and I drive the three miles across town to University Hospital, and I park at the emergency entrance on the north. While we wait for an attendant to come with a wheelchair, my mind and vision wander from University Hospital to the great, gleaming, private medical facility just across the street on Dewey Avenue.

This private medical facility across the street is one of the great healing institutions of the midwest. It has every convenience and service a hospital can offer. The staff is well-trained, capable, polite. The patient there is assured of the finest medical treatment and care now available in our society. I have often been there to visit patients or friends, and now and then I stop in at the attractive Coffee Shop and House of Gifts. That byway oasis, with its delicate atmosphere of gifts and fine things for patients, is a bit of respite and elegance in my otherwise inelegant life. The expensiveness, the care, the efficient orderliness, the way of the patient over the staff, all come to me as Ada and I wait in the emergency entrance of University Hospital.

There is one other thing that comes to my mind as we

wait. If Ada were entering the hospital across Dewey Avenue she would not be required to walk up a single step, for the entrance there is ground level. But if Ada were coming to University Hospital by bus, or if she were walking because she could not afford bus fare or the parking lot fee, she would walk up a flight of twenty-three steps to get to the emergency entrance from Dewey Avenue. Of course, she might walk around to the west ramp, but if she were coming by bus, as most patients do, she would take these steps, for they are the shortest way. These twenty-three enormous steps would be required of of her to enter this poor man's clinic, this Other World Hospital for the people of the Inner City.

Our entrance into the hospital itself is through heavy glass doors, which the patient must pull himself. Those doors do not revolve or open automatically. They must be pulled open with great effort. Once inside the hall I guide Ada down the corridor to the receiving desk. There is no soothing AM-FM music, coming from recessed speakers in the corridor; no figure of Christ welcomes the sick and the anxious; no nurse or attendant is on hand to help with the luggage or to greet the patient. These luxuries, so evident and taken for granted in the private facility just across Dewey Avenue, are frills nowhere to be seen or heard here at University.

The corridor is lined with the poor, the transient, the unskilled, the sick, and the helpless. They sit on chairs all along the wall. They stand when there are no more chairs. They wait patiently in wheelchairs, on crutches, and in walking frames. Some lean on others. A mother

61

holds her baby, surrounded by other crying children. Fathers and mothers shepherd their brood into out-of-the-way corners. Elderly women comfort their husbands, and elderly husbands speak reassuringly to their anxious wives. Pregnant teen-age girls stand in line, exposed to the scrutiny of all other patients. Whole families come for shots, for treatment, for diagnosis. Whites, blacks, Indians, Mexicans, Mixed couples and families, all mingle together in the corridors and side rooms and in every nook and cranny of University Hospital.

There is one bonding quality which cements all life and activity here in Receiving, one factor which makes a kind of Suffering Fellowship of all patients. That quality and factor is poverty. This poverty is not the temporary, hard-up kind of poverty, not the simple job layoff kind of poverty, not the set-back-that-will-soon-be-over kind of poverty. This is an ingrained, inherited, bone-shattering, soul-destroying, spirit-killing kind of poverty: poverty as a way of life.

It is poverty, not color, which makes the difference between University Hospital and the hospital just across Dewey Avenue. The difference is both in quality and in attitude of care. The sight of this endless stream of stricken humanity has its effect on the staff at University Hospital. That effect manifests itself in an urgency to process as many patients as possible, in the shortest time possible. It shows itself in an effort to provide a quantity of medical care at the expense of quality of that care.

I watch Ada as she moves forward in line toward Receiving. Ada knows about the hospital across the

street. She knows about Christ over the door, about the
Gift Shop, the way of the patient with the doctor, the
receptionist who carries the patient's luggage. Ada carries
her meager belongings in a brown paper sack. She stands
in a line where the infirm are held upright by friends. She
stands in a line where the deaf must ask someone to listen
for their names over the speaker. She stands in a line
where the blind must ask someone to guide them from
desk to desk, from line to line.

In this procession Ada joins with others in voiced
frustration about the interminable waiting. No part of
this hospital escapes the patient's scrutiny. It is voiced to
include doctors, nurses, technicians, custodians, and
clerks. Such goings-on by patients who have come to
claim free medical help may seem strange to tax-paying
observers, but what one hears in these lines—the con-
demnation and criticism—fulfills a need for these people.
This articulation of grievances is simply one of the
countless ways the disenfranchised of our society affirm
their dignity and independence. Ada knows quite well
that she will always be dependent on this hospital, and
on charity, but she wishes it were different. She wishes
she could afford the hospital across the street, but she
cannot, and so she maintains an air of independence because that independence is her sole hope of self-
respect.

Ada finally reaches the head of the line, is registered,
numbered, and given a chair. I sit beside her with words
of comfort and encourgement. We are not entirely at
ease with each other. We both know that I might very

63

well be mistaken for her son who will not provide his mother with private hospital care, even though he is quite capable of doing so. Ada is very sensitive about that. But after a time Ada's number is called over the speaker and we move toward the elevator to climb to Ward Five East. Down the hall we pass children of the poor who will grow up to produce children of the poor, forever dependent on free medical care. We pass side rooms where all manner of surgery and treatment are in progress. We pass wards of old people who will live out their lives in these rooms knowing they will never have a private doctor-patient relationship. They will live and die here as objects of intern curiosity.

We reach the desk at the entrance to Ward Five East. Ada's coming has been charted, her belongings are taken from her, and she is informed that she will change into a hospital gown and that her bed will be number 16. The nurses busily prepare themselves with papers and files and records, fussing to each other to hide the awkwardness of this moment of Ada's transformation from private person to charity patient.

It is time for me to go. Ada stands in the doorway of Ward Five East with nothing more to say. Her clouded eyes stare fixedly at me as she waits for one final note of hope. I take her hand and tell her that she is in good hands, that I pray for her, and that when I come back tomorrow she will be better. The tears in her eyes affirm her grief and isolation. I move away with a last gesture of friendship which is a wave of the hand. She is still standing with hospital gown across her arm, silent and alone,

64

as I turn the corner. I cannot look back because of my own grief.

I retrace my steps along the corridor, sick in my heart for all the Adas, and the children, and the pregnant young girls, of University Hospital. I could wish for bigger and better hospitals, for more discerning doctors and more sensitive nurses. Yet I know this is not entirely the answer to the Adas I know. Fixing a child's broken arm may do nothing to fix his broken spirit. X-raying an enlarged liver does not expose the ruptured soul. Cobalt kills cancer but it cannot kill hopelessness. There are life-giving medicines but few hurt-curing ones.

Someday beyond the buildings which are hospitals, beyond the research, treatment, and healing of bodies, beyond the discoveries of earth and planets. we will discover the causes of spirit sickness. We will, I dare to hope, someday know why these people become wards of the county and of the state in the first place, and we will learn to undo those patterns of life which keep the poor in poverty. We will learn *why* they remain patients, or outpatients, in all the University Hospitals of this nation.

I exit down the long corridor, past Receiving, toward Emergency. Tomorrow I will visit Ada again, and I think she will be better. But tonight I will pray for her and all those like her. I will somehow trust God to so work in all of us that there will be a time when these two worlds of healing will more nearly approximate each other. I must add the thought that because he is always the source of our healing, I have the feeling that somehow he may be causing it to happen even now.

EDIE AND SHERMAN

Edie and Sherman are two special friends of mine who were married in one of the churches I serve. Edie has a master's degree in education and teaches in one of the schools in the Inner City. Sherman is employed in Civil Service where he earns something like $10,400 per year. Sherman is quiet and confident while Edie is more outgoing and talkative. Both sing in the choir at church and have taught Sunday school. They both say that they would like to become more involved in the work of the church when their schedule will permit. Edie, Sherman, and I have been together a great many times over the years. They are in our home frequently and we are in theirs. We have dinner together, attend movies, and have developed a genuine appreciation for the four diverse individualities involved in such a relationship.

What sets Edie and Sherman apart from most other couples of this community is the fact of their interracial marriage. Edie is white, petite, small of stature. Sherman is very dark and big-boned. These facts of their physical appearance have been a factor in public response to them. It has been said of them many times that if only it were the other way around, Sherman white and Edie black, the problem would not be so acute. The saying of this, I think, is predicated on the premise that a white man has every right to a black girl, but that a white girl married to a black man is, well, something else.

They never escape the inquiring eye of society. Hostility and the desire-to-punish follow them everywhere—down the street, into their professional work, through their social and religious life, into every hotel, motel, beach, restaurant, and civic function they enter. They have been turned away from motels and hotels. They have been asked to leave theaters, have been isolated in restaurant corners, left off invitation lists, sent letters of filth, refused service in stores, had their meals over-salted on airline flights, been pushed off sidewalks, had waitresses deliberately spill food on them, been insulted from passing cars, and glared at every day of their lives.

A very small glimmer of insight into the enormity of this public reaction to Edie and Sherman comes to me on those occasions when I walk with a black mother to the hospital nursery room. Thinking me the father of the baby we have come to see, the nurses, staff, and visitors glower at us all across the nursery, whisper to co-workers and friends, and often avoid looking at us altogether.

Edie has been called so many insulting names, and Sherman has been degraded in so many ways, that I do not see how they stand it. They simply say that their love for each other is such that no one else can hurt them, or cause them to retaliate. I cannot understand how they manage to control their rage. I have difficulty controlling mine.

Edie and Sherman say there is no way to prepare oneself for an interracial marriage. Only their love, they say (and their remarkable good sense, it seems to me), carries them through. Their love is genuine and demonstrated easily. They feel they are able to go anywhere they choose in society although they do not, from a practical standpoint, do so. They are certain that the "changing climate of public opinion" is a real factor for the future of mixed marriages. They feel that their example can very well be a guide to other couples involved in interracial love and marriage. Even now, we are working together for the creation of an interracial fellowship which will provide counsel and support for couples going steady or already married.

I share without reservation the joy of Edie and Sherman's marriage. I weep for the agony society has caused these two precious persons. I agree that public opinion is changing and that in another generation or two the Edies and Shermans of our society will be accepted in a more complete way than they are now. I want this to happen because I see what it will mean to so many persons in this interracial parish.

But for Edie and Sherman this acceptance will be a long time coming. The "climate of public opinion" is now one of racism, hatred, suspicion, and ignorance with a vengeance. All the scars of this social "death wish" are upon Edie and Sherman. Only their love—mature and genuine—permits them to survive the onslaught of this cruelty. They suffer. The intensity and variety of their suffering are the tragedy elements in their lives. They are childless. Their marriage is without children because of a societal sterility. They live in a society which accepts the homosexual, the transvestite, the lesbian, and the drug addict more readily than the marriage between two persons, one black and one white. I think Edie and Sherman will have children sometime even though they say they feel the time is not right at the present. I am heartened by the fact that their marriage is not dependent on having children. Edie and Sherman will continue to be in love, kept together by affection and circumstance, and by their marvelous power of self-discipline.

When I pray for Edie and Sherman, for their friends and all the people of this parish, I know I pray about a sickness. That sickness is mortal in many cases, for those who shame themselves by their abuse of Edie and Sherman are nearly dead already. Those who have this sickness seem to see no place for the remedy of love. Their sickness seems to be almost terminal. Edie and Sherman are among those whose health and constitution are best and brightest.

—————— JERRY AND PEG ——————

One day near the middle of summer a black couple in this parish asked me if I would like to go house hunting with them. They had no particular reason for asking me except that we are good friends and share a good many things together. My feelings about them make them special people to me. Jerry and Peg are both employed, have a good combined income, and with their growing family needed a larger home to accommodate their family. They had made an appointment with a real estate firm, via telephone, to look at a particular home which had been listed in the newspaper. They called to ask if I might like to go with them, and I had to answer that I could not go at that particular time, but would it be possible for us to go at another time? A return call later in the day indicated that they had a new appointment to see the home late in the afternoon of the Fourth of July.

It was a hot and windy day they had chosen. Yet for all the heat and wind there was a kind of quietness upon the city, broken only by the sounds of fireworks prematurely detonated. American flags were flying everywhere along the street as we passed by. Family outings were to be seen in every park and on nearly every patio. Children roamed the streets, few cars broke the spell of jubilation, and dogs sauntered across the streets and avenues as if the streets and avenues were made for dogs. The flying flags, the noise of fireworks, the sounds of families, all celebrated the independence of a nation, the freeing of a people, the breaking of chains and the smashing of burdens. The joy and power of that event from so long ago in our national life is still very much with the American people.

The appointment was for 4:00. Peg and Jerry were dressed immaculately, as befits their pride in themselves. The real estate agent was to meet us at the house. As we drove leisurely through the suburban development we encountered the startled faces of families in yards and on sidewalks. Peg and Jerry are not at all bothered by the stares since they have been stared at all their lives. It bothers me, though, for I have never gotten accustomed to this form of hostility. All the homes we passed were well-kept ranch or Cape Cod designs, all giving form to the young executive-type nature of the community. They speak clearly of those middle-class values which so characterize this nation today. It was a manicured, orderly, well laid-out community, a platter so clean on the outside.

We reached our destination after some intricate maneuvering of the winding streets of the development, and parked at the curb in front of the house. In the driveway of the home with its two-car garage were the cars of the homeowner and the real estate agent. Peg, Jerry, and I left the car with rather forced conversation, conscious of our position at that moment. We were very careful not to walk on the lawn. On the landing step Jerry rang the doorbell. There was a silence from the house. As that silence deepened, there began to unfold a drama which you somehow expected to unfold but which you hoped to God would not. We waited, and after a while Jerry rang again. Any other time, in any other circumstance, the owner and the agent would have met us at the door before the doorbell could have been sounded. But not this time. The three of us knew without a word being spoken that a terrible drama was being enacted behind that front door. It was plain to us that before we came up the walk toward this house, neither agent nor homeowner had known that Jerry and Peg were black.

71

When the door did at last open, we were greeted by a nervously smiling man who identified himself as the owner, and we were invited inside. As we stood in the anteroom, just inside the front door, we caught a glimpse of the real estate agent and the homeowner's wife standing at the door near the rear entrance. The face of the agent was blanched and stricken. He did not come forward immediately.

In those moments there came to me the sensation of all of us being frozen, immobile, mesmerized by some time machine. We all stood gazing across some fathomless dividing line. There was the agent whose only contact with the prospective couple had been over the telephone. There were a confused homeowner and his wife, who never in all their lives dreamed of a situation like this. There were Jerry and Peg, caught up in one more of a seemingly endless procession of racial discriminations. There was a pastor who knew there was nothing he could say or do to have time begin again.

It was the remarkable Jerry who brought us all back into focus. Jerry moved forward toward the homeowner's wife and the agent, introduced himself and Peg and me, and commented on the beauty and arrangement of the house. The agent then began to respond with some alacrity, suggesting that the owner show us around and saying that he and the owner's wife would meet us later in the back yard.

The host, with presence and honesty, showed us the house. He explained some of the intricate details of each room, the construction, the furnishings, and the di-

72

mensions. He explained about the built-ins in the kitchen, the split-level nature of the living room, the fireplace. He was obviously proud of his home and proud to show it to us. But when he was finished and when there was nothing else to show, no more rooms to enter, the time of reckoning descended upon us. He suggested we meet his wife and the agent on the patio.

At the rear of the house in a cool and shady oasis of yard we met again the agent and homeowner's wife. They had both regained their composure, but there was a tenseness and a feeling of overwhelming suspicion in the air. Each member of that drama knew we were being watched from offstage through window lattices and from beyond hedgerows. All the talk about Negroes moving into the community focused on this one household on a holiday afternoon.

The real estate agent began to question Peg and Jerry about the home. Was it adequate, was it comfortable, could they be happy in it? When Jerry replied that it was all this, the agent began to explain about the cost, the mortgage payments, the closing costs. When Jerry and Peg agreed that they could afford this, the agent moved at last to the long-delayed salient point of his position. There were no other colored in the neighborhood! It might be difficult for Jerry's family to be the only Negro family here, and it might even be difficult for the other families in the neighborhood. The agent said he wanted to level with them, and he knew they realized his position; that it wasn't a question of being prejudiced (after all, some of his best friends were Negroes), it was just that neighbors can sometimes make it difficult for folks who move in, and he wouldn't want that to happen to Jerry and Peg. The agent concluded by saying that perhaps Jerry and Peg ought to talk it over for a few days and let him know their decision.

The fact is that their decision had already been made. Jerry and Peg wanted to buy the house. The agent did then what he knew he had to do. He explained without hesitation that another family which had looked at the house had asked the owner not to sell until they could come back for another look. The agent said he knew that the owner and his wife wanted to be considerate to this other family. "Tell you what," the agent said genially to the owner, "why don't you let me know right away when you hear from this other family? If they decide not to take the house, I will call these fine folks here and we will come back and talk some more about the details. Do you folks think that would be all right?"

Jerry asked if they had any idea low long that might be. "Oh, these things take time you know. It might be several weeks. But I promise you I will let you know the minute we have something from this other family. I believe that's the way we ought to leave it. How about it, folks, is that all right with you?"

This question, put to so many Negroes over the years, in so many situations just like this one, can have but one answer. Open housing laws are an important move toward changing the answer, but until there is greater enforcement of such laws, and greater change of attitude

74

on the part of white Americans, the answer will be foreordained.

The ride back to Jerry's and Peg's was not a strained one especially, but there was a somberness which we could not shake. There was laughter along the way, but underneath I felt the humiliation and anger of these people who were so dear to me. I wondered how much of the humiliation would turn to hate. I wondered how much love they would have to pour on the humiliation to keep it from changing to hate. I could not know because I was not Peg or Jerry, and I am not a Negro.

The house was not sold for months. No call came. Jerry and Peg looked elsewhere and finally bought a house in another development. The three of us talked about this incident many times in the ensuing months. All of us tried to analyze our emotions and feelings, and I believe that out of it came some deeper insights into the whys and the ways of our reactions and human feelings.

I remember this experience well. But most of all I remember, on that great American holiday, celebrated with speeches, commemorations, and the sounding of fireworks, how gracefully the flags of freedom flapped and waved in the afternoon air.

———— *WILLIAM SMITH* ————

William Smith is a Baptist minister friend of mine who serves a church not far from this parish. He is a graduate of one of the best seminaries in the country. On the wall of his study are certificates acknowledging him to be an outstanding student, preacher, and continuing scholar. He serves an all-black church. He has a gracious wife and active family and a rather high level of income.

William Smith and I move around together in the Inner City. We go to meetings together occasionally, meet for mid-morning coffee, or have lunch every now and then. We have met in our respective studies for conversation and prayer (frequently on our knees, in good Baptist fashion). William Smith is a powerful speaker and completely dedicated to the Lord. In some ways I envy him. One of the reasons I envy him is that he is very confident of himself and his identity.

He believes he understands both whites and blacks perfectly. I do not have this certainty. I am not always sure that what I *think* about blacks and whites is what is *true* about blacks and whites. William and I talk about this at different times and he is sure he knows the basic instincts of both blacks and whites. For this reason he is certain that the Black Church must become a separate reality in American society. William Smith enjoys our relationship, he says. He takes specific steps to cultivate it, and insists that our congregations cooperate in various ventures. Yet he has no hesitation in saying that before there can be true integration of churches there must first be complete separation of churches. His feeling is that whites will never accept blacks into meaningful spiritual fellowship until those blacks have developed significant churches and responsible lay leadership in their all-black congregations.

I disagree with William about this. I disagree not only because other black ministers disagree with him, but because one of the churches I serve is, I believe, an example of how an integrated church does succeed. This church has black leadership at every level. It is, in membership and in leadership, more black than white. To me, it is an example of an integrated church that works.

William does not agree. He believes that even though whites might very well move into a meaningful white-black relationship in the church, the blacks are psychologically in a precarious position because most of them have not had opportunity for leadership in the black church. William believes whites now condescend to blacks out of respect to the Black Movement more than because they freely and without reservation accept the blacks as persons.

Sometimes I *think* William is right, but I am not *certain* he is right. The main thing I try to do is learn from him. It is this effective man of God, black and energetic, who leads us both through many a memorable moment. In his study he leans back in his swivel chair and sometimes ignores me altogether. There are times when he turns his back on me and examines the books on his library shelf, or shuffles papers on his desk, opens his mail, or watches a spider crawl up the wall. These moments are baffling to me, but by word and gesture I know he is shutting me out, putting me out of his mind, closing the door to a white man who intrudes into his black world. I chide him for his rudeness, and we both laugh.

On one occasion he explained that whites are searchers after identity in a way far more profound than are blacks. This is especially so when whites move into the black community. There, William believes, whites are wanderers in a strange land; they are interlopers among an alien race. William has reminded me that blacks move in and out of white society with ease, since they have been required to do this since the earliest days of slavery. But whites have not yet been able to feel at home in blackland, William says. Because white entry into the black community is only of recent origin, William says, that entry is an uncertain one. I think I denied that once, in all honesty, but now I have learned too much about myself to deny it any longer. I sit in William's study, in a relationship which is meaningful for both of us, but he can still sit with his back to me, and I can very easily wait for him to turn again.

William shares a great many insights about white Inner City workers. These insights reveal him to be a man of profound judgment. He knows nearly all the professionals who work in the Inner City. He has the conviction that a great many of them are phony when it comes to fundamental identification with other people. However dedicated these white professional workers are to The Cause, William sees many of these workers as more interested in their air-conditioned offices, and in their filing systems, than they are in any attempt to carry the burdens of the poor.

William sees how many of these professionals find their identity in the Inner City in terms of dress, patois, and mannerism. He will say bluntly that a great many white Inner City workers seek a relation to blacks because they have not been able to relate to their white contemporaries. William feels very strongly that blacks neither expect, nor respect, such false identity. The drive of the Negro today is for identification, and he has little love for the man, white or black, who purposely gives up his identity as a white or as a black.

When William Smith preaches, he shakes the beams of his wood-frame church. When he articulates his philosophy of separatism-before-integration, he shakes a good many whites. When he turns his back to me I go on talking, and he goes on listening, and I do not always know what I say or what I hears. I do know William Smith is for real. He is a real person in color, integrity, and purpose. He provides leadership in the Inner City which is stable and enduring. He has an initiative which I envy. He is one of my teachers in the Inner City.

CLEO

Cleo Juliard is a black woman from the Mississippi Delta who thinks she is about ninety years old. I think she is at least that, and maybe more. She is tough as nails, gifted with a sense of humor, and possesses a courage that makes me ashamed of myself. Cleo lives in a public housing project on something like $96 a month. She says she hasn't seen a doctor in more than five years. Medicine is prescribed for her over the telephone from the Welfare Department. Now and then she buys some old-fashioned drugstore remedy she believes will "Clean her out." She chews tobacco, reads her bible every day, swears very choice words, some of them current four-letter ones.

Cleo never went to school a day in her life, can read some but not write much, and has more native sense than most people I know. She remembers everything about yesterday but cannot remember much of today. She laughs uproariously when she tells me about the time she tried to kill a turtle for the family pot. She hammered nails into it, tried to burn it, finally cut it up with an ax. She likes apples, beets, and chitlins. Her little apartment in the Project smells like old bacon grease, but it is filled with little things of Cleo's life that make it a sanctuary for her. She is apprehensive about men. She is not afraid of me, but she is sometimes uncertain about me when I fail to say plainly what I mean. She has never been to the church I serve in the community, but she knows the Lord loves her, and there is no doubt in her mind that she will go to heaven when she dies. That is a prospect which becomes more and more appealing to Cleo as the days go by.

Cleo is a nearly forgotten member of the human family, a commentary on life in our society. She is a living reminder that some Americans still live in bondage. There is a convergence of things about Cleo. Indifference to the plight of the aged, indifference to the plight of the blacks, a soothing-of-conscience when we have provided nearly helpless persons with a little room, some food and medicine, are all reflected in Cleo. She is nothing more, in the sight of this society, than the backwash of the race, a backwash in a clear, moving stream of plenty.

One day I sat with Cleo on the back step of her little place in the Project. The rear entrance to her apartment leads out onto the third-floor landing. A rusty iron rail encircles this small alcove above the ground, and our two chairs nearly filled the small space. We sat together on a warm day in September. Around us on every side were the apartments of the Project. Windows everywhere were open, and the sounds, sights, and smells of congestion moved across our sensory landscapes. Below us skittered the apartment dwellers, going to and fro in hurried nonchalance. Our conversation was mostly about Cleo.

"Cleo," I asked, when the conversation was drawing to a close, "do you have many regrets about life?"

She thought for a moment before she answered, her face turning in every direction as if surveying the contours of her life. When she answered, it was a breezy and earthy reply, expressed in the dialect of her Mississippi heritage.

"I regret most everything. Ain't never been a day I didn't regret. I regret being' born, I regret havin' kids, the only thing I won't ever regret is dyin'. Ain't no damm good livin' in this world. Ain't had nothin' except bein' hungry and poor. Seems like a body can't do nothin' in this world without somebody poopin' on him. Like once I asked a white man to call me a doctor for one of my sick children. He said nigger children all better off dead. I think he's damm right. All my children dead and they better off'n I am."

She eyed the iron rail with a jaundiced and practiced eye. She had no tobacco but she eyed the rail in anticipation. "Cleo," I said, "what have you liked best about life?"

She waited again and watered her mouth, and had she had her tobacco I think she would have spit a bucketful in every direction. With a marvelous light which I so often see in this great woman's eyes, she answered my question.

"I like folks what lives next to me. All the folks I don't like live somewheres else. Seems to me I like just about everything excep'n folks what think they bigger than God."

Cleo turned in her chair and faced me with a burning look. "Reverend, you and me and folks like us got everything we need. Ain't nothin' the Lord don't give. We got to be humble and let the Lord do what he wants."

Cleo and I had prayer together on this cramped veranda. We sat and talked some more after that, and when it was time to go I held out my hand and she held out hers. But in that position, with two hands extended in some kind of understanding, hands suddenly became inadequate. So, I stepped forward spontaneously and put my arms around her. In an awkward response she returned the embrace. I was soon gone, but I remember the feel of this ninety-year-old woman. She felt like a bag of bones, which she is. But, in an incomparable way, she also felt like a soft bird's song from the long night's stillness.

————— *TAYLOR* —————

I first met Taylor Lincoln at a Black Power meeting held a few days after the rioting in Omaha during the summer of 1969. It was a meeting of people who had come together to talk about and digest the events of the past week. There was violent talk in this meeting, conciliatory talk, white talk and black talk. Neither whites nor blacks had any clear-cut idea of what to do next, or how to undo what had already been done.

Taylor did not speak much at this informal gathering of North-Side people, but what he did say was clear and to the point. He was not in favor of burning down the city. He was not in favor of character assassination or a vendetta against whites. He was not, in fact, greatly interested in what his fellow blacks had to say, and not at all interested in what whites had to say. The truth is that Taylor Lincoln has his own program of Black Power, and it is the project which occupies him almost exclusively. Taylor Lincoln is determined to bring about changes in society through the difficult, time-consuming, but long-range effective method of educating black children. These changes are not to take place in or through the present educational process, but beyond that process in strange and radical ways. At least they are strange and radical to a great many persons who look to these ways with horror.

Taylor Lincoln has no wish to publicize his methods of reaching these black children. This austere silence is in keeping with the character of Taylor Lincoln. He is a second-year student in the state university in this city. He is twenty years old, six feet tall, wears a beard, an Afro haircut, and has his clothes tailor-made. He is studying to be a social worker and is a dedicated student. Taylor is enrolled at the university under a variety of grants provided by community and private agencies. He lives at home with his mother in a comfortable, well-kept home on the North Side. He does not support violence. He thinks the idea of burning down buildings is stupid and childish. His efforts toward change are far more subtle and sinuous.

Taylor Lincoln is a part of a dedicated corps of young blacks, mostly male, who have zeroed in on the elementary public school system as the place to effect long-range social change. Jason Street School is one target of this effort. Taylor himself does not say much about what he and others are doing at this point, but among the many sources of information there is to be gleaned some salient features of this effort.

Jason Street School is in a badly neglected part of the city. The children attending here are largely black, although there are some whites as well. It is the third oldest school building in the city. The massive oak doors, painted a dozen different colors over the years, hang forbiddingly from black metal frames. The rooms of this

84

school have high ceilings, the floors have been sanded and oiled almost to the joists, and the playground equipment is old and colorless. There is no grass on the lawns, only scrubby and tracked-down water grass.

Taylor Lincoln and a small corps of workers see in the Jason Street Schools of this nation the real battleground of the future. The victories to be won must be won in the hearts of children, and these victories come through concentrated efforts of reeducation. On any typical day of the school year, Taylor, or members of his group, can be found on the sidewalks which feed the children to and from Jason Street School. These young workers walk these sidewalks casually, seemingly without direction, but with an inward purpose. What takes place on those sidewalks is an exchange of conversation with children. It is always a one-to-one encounter. The words spoken by Taylor or his friends will depend on the child and the situation. Sometimes the words are soft and comforting. Other times they are harsh and frightening. They are all provocative.

"Hi there, black boy!"

"Hi," or, "Hello." Or nothing. (Black mothers warn their children about strangers just like every other mother).

"You like school?"

"Yes," or, "No." Or nothing. (Black kids can play dumb, too).

"Are you proud to be black?" A "yes" more likely than not.

"Black is better than white, isn't it?"

"I guess so." Or nothing. (Black children aren't at all sure about that).

"White kids call you 'nigger,' don't they?"

"Yes." That hits home every time.

"Your mother is black, isn't she?" The answer is "yes."

"You love your mother, don't you?" The answer is "yes."

"Are you proud of her?" The answer is "yes."

"She's better than a white mother, isn't she?"

"I guess so."

"You'll be a great man some day, won't you?" Mostly the answer to this is, "I don't know." They really don't know about that. Eight or nine is an uncertain age to be thinking about greatness.

"You will be, boy, because you're black. Black is the best color there is for greatness. Right, man?"

"Right." He doesn't understand it, but it's in his mind.

Other workers from this group may approach the child in a different tone of voice.

"You hate whites?" No, or yes.

"Do you know whites hate you?" No, or yes.

"You better watch out, black boy. Whites are going to kill you!"

Sometimes it is more suggestion than question.

"Stay away from whites!"

"Tell your mama your white teacher molested you."

Taylor Lincoln knows the children react in various ways. But because he is black himself, he knows the fertile field of hurt in the psyche of every black child. To an extent which Taylor knows best, these black children respond with an unconscious agreement born of all the times they have been called "nigger," beaten up by white gangs, made an object of scorn by a white teacher, cursed, ignored, or abused. Taylor knows quite well that all this takes its toll in these young lives.

Taylor knows that whites are alarmed by all this. He knows whites are afraid of what all this might lead to. But Taylor Lincoln does not swerve from his task. He remembers. He remembers the abuse, the cursings, the hurt. Taylor knows that Black Power gains momentum because it is fed by white violence. I remember that the children of Jason Street School are very young, and that the full weight of their opinions and convictions will not bear fruit for another ten or fifteen years. I do not know where Taylor Lincoln and his corps of dedicated young men are taking us. I do know that their efforts may very well presage the coming of a long, hot generation.

AFTERWORD

As an Inner City worker I am asked to do a great many things. I am asked to perform abortions, get drugs for addicts, booze for alcoholics, go to Kansas City or Denver or Tulsa, talk to someone, get a lawyer, find a witness, get some money, locate a runaway daughter. I cannot go to those places, I seldom get the money, the witnesses are never there, the lawyers want their fee first, and the daughters almost always come home.

Yet one of the hardest things for me to do in my role as an Inner City clergyman is to "give a program." Requests for speaking engagements come from groups who want to know about the Inner City, and I have the conviction that I ought to do what I can to provide such information. When I do speak to groups I do my best to give factual, honest interpretations of Inner City life and people. I suggest that members of these groups read the Report of the National Advisory Commission on Civil Disorders. I suggest they join any number of interracial fellowship groups to be found in the city. They can worship in black churches, join black churches, identify with black efforts, and support black causes. They can witness to the love of God by engaging in honest communication with persons of minority groups. I speak of personal involvement in a great many Inner City or metropolitan interracial programs. I spell out the opportunities available.

Sometimes members of the groups to which I speak respond with an open willingness to learn and participate. Other times they simply want me to reassure them that there will be no more riots, that blacks will stay in their place, that a little bit of money will pacify the poor. I cannot provide any such reassurance.

I do hold up the church as a powerful agent of reconciliation. I also promote the church as an undiscovered, unused instrument of tremendous potential in service to persons. I look at the figures today which explain the unit cost of helping the poor, and I shudder. Nearly $10,000 has been spent by one anti-poverty agency in this city in sewing classes. The number of women enrolled in this program was something like twelve. Those same women could have been taught to sew in nearly every church in this city for $250. The only cost would have been equipment and supplies. The supervision would have cost nothing. That supervision would have come from volunteers who know more about sewing than most of those on the agency staff. Indeed, this kind of supervision is being given daily in a great many churches of this city, including one of the churches I serve. It costs neither the federal government, the state, nor the city. It is done for love.

Every day this past summer, members of the Neighborhood Youth Corps have passed by the church on their way to work. These young men and women earn money by hoeing weeds, mowing grass, picking up trash, cleaning vacant lots, and painting old buildings. Much of the work is a lark, and the young people know it. At

89

the end of the summer they have earned some money, they have brightened a few buildings and killed off a few patches of weeds. But they have not been given a skill for that investment, a skill which will serve them usefully in the coming years.

Long before there was a Peace Corps, long before there was VISTA or OEO or NYC, there was in this country a significant network of church-related, youth-oriented service programs. The young people who committed themselves to these programs were trained and equipped to serve in a multitude of places throughout the world. They worked for little remuneration. They did agricultural work, supervised farm animal programs, implemented vocational and technical training enterprises, instructed native peoples in the arts of irrigation, fertilization, and crossbreeding of animals and grains, and demonstrated the possibilities of increased production through methods of conservation. They taught children the basics of reading, writing and arithmetic, trained leaders in youth programs, built schools, gave sewing and cooking lessons, explained menu planning and nutrition needs, and assisted in setting up teaching sessions in hygiene, home economics, and family planning. These young people gave years of their lives to worthwhile things, and when they returned home they had skills, a sense of accomplishment and dignity, and an appreciation for the people of the world.

I believe this is what young people, by and large, want and need in the Inner City. It is a framework of experiences which the church can help provide. It is, as a matter of fact, a framework of experiences which the church is providing now, and which could be vastly enlarged and strengthened with increased support. If a working relationship could be established between the federal government and present church-related youth ventures in service, young people from the Inner City could be trained on docks, farms, forests, mountains, and deserts. Such training could involve work with children, young people, families, the sick, the institutionalized, the elderly, and the isolated. This skill-training program could be conducted through the present network of service projects of the church, and it could be done quite apart from any sectarian or "religious" framework.

The church, with its present administrative organization and its past experience, could give the youth of our cities employment, involvement, and lasting skills. The church has schools, institutes, vocational academies, camps, health clinics, rehabilitation programs, agricultural missions, and educational facilities, to provide nearly every form of training and service required of this society. These agencies are staffed by trained and dedicated people. The church has, in addition, one extra ingredient which makes this approach so very exciting. It has a motivation for service which is so paramount in any venture of this kind. That motivation is genuine love of persons.

I think the church is ready to be used in this effort. I believe the church could be used in this effort. I wish the Department of Labor would discover the church.

These are some of the things I say when I speak of my work in the Inner City and of the needs of people there. When those to whom I speak respond with meaningful appreciation, I thank God for his power to touch and move the hearts of persons. When those to whom I speak respond with indifference or hostility, I pray that God might work in some new way beyond myself to show them the way. I never underestimate the power of God. I have been in the Inner City far too long to make such a foolish mistake.

Not many days ago the Peace and Freedom Party held a public rally in a park not far from one of the churches of this parish. Speakers at this rally directed their remarks at the President of the United States, the governor of this state, the mayor of this city, and a variety of other public officials who were all described together as "pig racists." The call of this rally was for the overthrow of the national government, for the redistribution of all national wealth among minorities and the poor, and for the placing of police power in the hands of local neighborhoods.

I understand deeply the anguish and frustration of these men. I understand how desperately they work for anything which they believe will relieve the plight and condition of their soul brothers. I know something of the heritage of these blacks who have suffered such monstrous wrongs at the hands of white Americans. I know they carry these wrongs very close to the core of their conduct and action. I am so identified with their desperation, so responsive to their feelings of rage, that I am never free from the temptation to join their desperate methods.

But I cannot do it. For all my involvement in the power movements of the Inner City, I cannot give up the strong conviction that to resort to violence is to negate what small benefits are accrued from that violence. My first concern is for the spirit of men, and that extends to the violator as well as to the violated. No man strengthens his spirit by destroying the spirit of others. Revenge, for whatever cause, only creates the need for more revenge. There is a better way. No movement, no cause, no agency, no person, contributes to the final achievement of human rights and human dignity if he approaches that task with malice.

But the Inner City clergyman, the social worker, the concerned citizen, remembers that he labors in a cause of freedom which is of the spirit as well as of the body. He remembers that this desired freedom for a minority will mean nothing finally if even one person is enslaved to a dividing hostility. It is in the humanizing of our motives and our actions that our victory lies. This is a lesson which I have had to learn again and again from my black brothers in the ministry. We labor together in a cause which seeks to lift up the spirit of men as well as break down the chains of men. We labor together in a cause which has as its utimate goal the bringing together of all men everywhere in a fellowship which has no room for rancor or rage. There are times when this goal seems to be within the realm of possibility.

Such is the life and drama of this parish. These are my teachers in the Inner City. I learn from each of them. They are never away from my mind. Connie, Joe, Benny, Taylor, William, Cleo, are the human figures in the celebration of life here. There are many more, both in this book and in this parish, who make this celebration a never-ending adventure. I watch and pray. I grow and change. I wait with a mixture of hope and foreboding. I give myself as a part of this hope.